MW00366295

This journal belongs to:

....

LOIS EVANS

Seasons
OF A WOMAN'S LIFE
DEVOTIONAL JOURNAL

HARVEST HOUSE PUBLISHERS
EUGENE, OREGON

SEASONS OF A WOMAN'S LIFE DEVOTIONAL JOURNAL

Text copyright © 2013 by Lois Evans

Published by Harvest House Publishers

Eugene, Oregon 97402

www.harvesthousepublishers.com

ISBN 978-0-7369-5320-7

Design and production by Franke Design & Illustration, Excelsior, Minnesota

Adapted from *Seasons of a Woman's Life* by Lois Evans, copyright © 2000 Lois Evans.

Used by permission of Moody Publishers.

Unless otherwise indicated, all Scripture quotations are from the New King James Version.

Copyright © 1982 by Thomas Nelson, Inc. Used by permission. All rights reserved.

Verses marked NIV are taken from the Holy Bible, New International Version®, NIV®.

Copyright © 1973, 1978, 1984, 2011, by Biblica, Inc.™ Used by permission of Zondervan.

All rights reserved worldwide. www.zondervan.com

All rights reserved. No part of this publication may be reproduced, stored in
a retrieval system, or transmitted in any form or by any means—electronic, mechanical,
digital, photocopy, recording, or any other—except for brief quotations in printed reviews,
without the prior permission of the publisher.

Printed in China

13 14 15 16 17 18 19 / RDS / 10 9 8 7 6 5 4 3 2 1

A Journey Through Many Seasons

God has blessed me with wonderful opportunities to speak to women—
women of all ages, races, and social status. When I'm able to talk to
these women one-on-one, I am privileged to hear about their wishes,
their wants, and their worries. I hear their longings for blessing—blessings
for their families as well as for themselves. I hear the cry of their hearts
because of unexpected disappointments, heartaches, and frustrations.
And I hear the same question asked in many different ways. Whatever
their age, whatever their responsibilities, women want to know,
Will it always be like this?

The answer to that question is almost always no. You've heard the saying
"All things must pass." Though it's true, at least in earthly terms, there's a
more specific principle at work than that. Women are seasonal creatures,
and when we look at our lives in light of the season we are in,
we are better able to cope with some of the challenges, more likely
to appreciate the blessings, and move forward.

In the pages that follow, you'll find helpful principles and encouraging
promises to explore and write about. Together, we'll consider the kind of
seeds God is planting in our hearts, the type of growth He anticipates,
and the abundant harvest He expects from us as He leads us through the
seasons of our lives. For He has said, "I know the thoughts that I think
toward you...thoughts of peace and not of evil, to give you a future
and a hope" (Jeremiah 29:11).

—*Lois Evans*

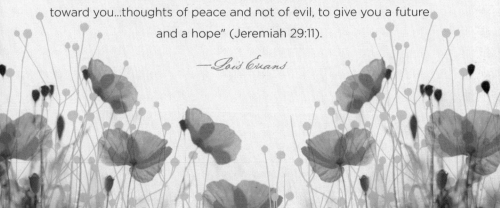

*I*t is essential for us to learn about our seasons because God has a unique plan for each of us. The Bible says that God ordered our days before we were ever born, and when we submit to His unique path, He will help us keep our balance and navigate the many choices in life.

Seek to maintain a vital personal relationship with God, be the best you can be no matter what field of service God has called you to, and learn to use your privileged position to further the cause of Christ in the world.

By doing this, you will "let your light so shine before men, that they may see your good works and glorify your Father in heaven."

_____

_____

_____

_____

_____

_____

_____

_____

_____

_____

_____

_____

_____

_____

_____

_____

_____

_____

Your eyes saw my unformed body; all the days ordained for me
were written in your book before one of them came to be.

PSALM 139:16 NIV

What's your story? How are you using your privileged position for God?

An ongoing awareness of His presence
and a devotion to His Word give us
stability, confidence, and direction.

The first seed that is planted in the heart of a godly woman is the seed of God's call. Every woman who walks with the Lord has a different story to tell about how God reached out and drew her to Himself.

He calls us because He loves us. He calls us because, before the foundation of the world, each of us was foreseen and designed in every intricate detail.

You are not a chance happening. You are one of a kind. There is no one else on this planet who has your plan. Because you are more than a conqueror in Jesus Christ, you can relax in the face of trouble and temptation.

"For I know the plans I have for you," declares the LORD, "plans to prosper you and not to harm you, plans to give you hope and a future."

JEREMIAH 29:11 NIV

How did God reach out and draw you to Himself?

*O*nce you answer His loving call at the
point of salvation, you enter into that
glorious, divine plan devised especially
for you by your sovereign God.

Because we've received Jesus Christ, we are joint heirs with Him. If we live life focusing on who we are—God's heirs—we can get through the difficult times because there is hope. There is joy ahead. There is a promise waiting to be fulfilled.

When desperate needs come up, we must not forget who we are and to whom we belong. Since we've responded to His call, the Lord can take care of our problems. He can even use the bad and the ugly issues of our past and begin weaving them together into His kingdom plan. So, live every day knowing that you are His child and that something good is going to come out of your difficult circumstances.

The Spirit Himself bears witness with our spirit that we are
children of God, and if children, then heirs—heirs of God and
joint heirs with Christ, if indeed we suffer with Him,
that we may also be glorified together.

ROMANS 8:16-17

How does God's heir—a joint heir with Christ—act in the face of life's difficult situations? Does your behavior reflect that truth?

....
....
....
....
....
....
....
....
....
....
....
....
....
....
....
....
....
....
....

Place all your confidence in an all-knowing God.

The Lord has a divine purpose for those He calls to Himself and has designed them to use their gifts, talents, and skills to promote His kingdom. God does more than call us into salvation. He calls us into His service. Salvation offers us a new purpose in history.

God's call is a compulsion you just can't shake. Answer Him by saying, "Yes, Lord!" and stop worrying. Whatever His call requires of you, He will provide you with the resources and orchestrate the people, places, and things in our lives to get the job done. What's more, you will experience the matchless joy of knowing that you are right where you belong.

As we focus on Him, He steers us into His perfect will.

Trust in the Lord with all your heart, and lean not on your
own understanding; in all your ways acknowledge Him,
and He shall direct your paths.

PROVERBS 3:5-6

*A*re you avoiding something God has called you to? Talk it over with your Christian friends. Ask God for confirmation, and step forward.

Our call is an invitation into a uniquely
designed life role, a role that God has
equipped us to carry out.

To effectively respond to our calling, we must walk with God on a daily basis and build ourselves up in His Word. This prepares us for the unknown, unpredictable, and unexpected events that come along. By storing up the Word in our hearts and building strong confidence in our all-knowing God, we learn to trust Him implicitly and obey Him without doubts or questions.

God's Word includes everything we need to know about life. It continually reminds us that the One who can save us can also keep us. He has promised to fulfill the desires of our heart. He knows exactly what we need and how much of any given season is enough.

Do your best to present yourself to God as one approved,
a worker who does not need to be ashamed and who
correctly handles the word of truth.

2 TIMOTHY 2:15 NIV

How are you coping with today's stresses in this current season? What Scripture verse gives you comfort in times of distress?

....

....

....

....

....

....

....

....

....

....

....

....

....

....

....

....

....

....

....

....

In God's grace, we are given only
what we can handle.

Whatever your season, whatever your call, please don't be willful. And don't try to do anything in your own power. God's strength is made perfect in your weakness. Though these are not popular ideas in our culture, for the woman who knows and loves her Lord, listening to God, waiting for His call, allowing Him to be her strength, and choosing to fulfill her seasons are choices that are deeply gratifying. Nothing is more rewarding than being in God's will and experiencing His peace.

To accomplish what God has planned for you, read His Word and fellowship with His people. Also, find a mentor who is wise in the ways of the Lord. Each of us needs someone to encourage us when God's call comes.

And He said to me, "My grace is sufficient for you, for My strength is made perfect in weakness." Therefore most gladly I will rather boast in my infirmities, that the power of Christ may rest upon me.

2 CORINTHIANS 12:9

When the Lord looks at you, what does He see? Does He see someone He can use?

The road won't always be easy, but God will never leave you; and, as you move through the seasons of your life, He will not be silent.

*J*ust as our earthly lives require discipline, diligence, and determination, a committed spiritual life requires the same, plus full dependence on Him. We must get to know Him and the power of His resurrection. Only then will we be able to face life's demands and our own fears.

Though we will always be vulnerable to the pressures of the world and the temptations of the flesh, God's Word makes it abundantly clear who is in charge of the outcome. "You are of God, little children, and have overcome them, because He who is in you is greater than he who is in the world" (1 John 4:4).

Commitment involves taking risks, and risks reveal the power of God. Once you've seen the awesome power of God at work in your life, never again will you doubt His capability to help you.

....
....
....
....
....
....
....
....
....
....
....
....
....
....
....
....
....
....

Fear not, for I am with you; be not dismayed, for I am your God.
I will strengthen you, yes, I will help you, I will uphold you with
My righteous right hand.

ISAIAH 41:1

Describe a time you felt overwhelmed by a specific commitment. What did you learn about God as you fulfilled that commitment?

....

....

....

....

....

....

....

....

....

....

....

....

....

....

....

....

....

....

....

....

*W*hen storms arise, we can look to our source of strength for the sustenance to make it through.

Communion with God is the source from which all our strength flows. Communion means intimate fellowship and deep relationship. At the cross we were bought with a price, and at the point of salvation, we were introduced to the One who bought us. We must find out how to call on the One who bought us and how to read His directions for a godly life.

If we want to reap the full benefits of our life in Christ, we have to know Him. We can only know Him by spending time in His Word and in prayer. Communion with God does not happen by chance. It is a decision of the will.

Call to Me, and I will answer you, and show you great and
mighty things, which you do not know.

JEREMIAH 33:3

Do you make communion with God a top priority? Are you seeing His mighty hand at work in your life?

....

....

....

....

....

....

....

....

....

....

....

....

....

....

....

....

....

....

....

....

The more time we spend with Jesus,
the more we come to understand why
we need Him every hour of every day.

Sometimes the seasons of our lives seem to be at a standstill. We can feel stuck as we wait for young children to grow, a better job to come our way, or an illness to pass. What should we do?

Look into Jesus' face and trust Him to make the path clear. As a child of God, allow Him to work out every aspect of your life—in His time. To wait on the Lord means to be patient and quiet while He is at work. In His presence—in that secret place to which He has called us—He helps us understand the importance of patience, the value of rest in Him, and the eternal significance of staying in the center of His will.

But those who wait on the LORD shall renew their strength; they shall mount up with wings like eagles, they shall run and not be weary, they shall walk and not faint.

ISAIAH 40:31

What are you waiting for? What is God teaching you about waiting and resting in Him?

....

....

....

....

....

....

....

....

....

....

....

....

....

....

....

....

....

....

In the privacy of the secret place, God is doing some deep work inside of you. He is allowing His Spirit to flow through you.

As Christian women, our spiritual growth depends on our health, and our health depends on our obedience to God's rules. We can never bloom into our full potential unless we are obedient. This season of growth is a special time in our lives when we go through an intense process of obedience, service, and preparation for the future God has designed us for. And it's rarely easy.

You may have to wrestle with unruly emotions and overcome prejudices and preconceived notions, but by humbling ourselves before God and pleading with Him for the strength to carry on, He will grow us into the obedient women we want to become and He desires us to be.

If you love Me, keep My commandments.

JOHN 14:15

Describe a time when obedience was difficult for you. What was God asking you to do? Why was it hard to obey?

We obey God so that we can cooperate with His work within us. Because He loves us, He wants us to be more like Him. He is growing us up in grace.

*O*bedience is a choice. Obeying is rarely the easy or popular thing to do. To obey the Master seems, sometimes, to make no sense at all. But once we seriously reflect upon who He is and what He can do in our lives, we find a way to make the adjustment.

God is trustworthy, holy, and all-powerful. He has a heart full of love for you. And He has your future written into His plans for the universe. He will take care of you. He will give you more than you could ask for in ways that are in accordance with His Word. When you have a trusting relationship with God, you will be able to confidently obey Him.

"The Lord is my portion," says my soul, "therefore I hope in Him!" The Lord is good to those who wait for Him, to the soul who seeks Him.

LAMENTATIONS 3:24-25

When you surrender your will and obey God, how does that impact your future decisions? Why?

....

....

....

....

....

....

....

....

....

....

....

....

....

....

....

....

....

....

If the Lord is your Shepherd, then obey
Him and count on Him to meet your needs.

Although obedience has a price, the rewards are wonderful. If you will obey and trust the Lord, He will take care of you. God chooses not to reveal everything to us. Of the things He has revealed, these we know to be true: He always wants us to remember that He is God, He wants us to submit to Him, and He wants us to trust and obey Him just as Jesus did.

When Jesus learned to obey even through suffering, He learned it for us—to teach us and to save us. "Though He was a Son, yet He learned obedience by the things which He suffered. And having been perfected, He became the author of eternal salvation to all who obey Him" (Hebrews 5:8-9).

The secret things belong to the Lᴏʀᴅ our God, but those things which are revealed belong to us and to our children forever, that we may do all the words of this law.

DEUTERONOMY 29:29

What price have you recently paid to obey God? What was your reward?

....

....

....

....

....

....

....

....

....

....

....

....

....

....

....

....

....

....

....

....

God speaks to us constantly, but if we're
not familiar with His voice, we will obey
our own instead.

There's no question about it. If we're going to follow Jesus Christ, we are going to be servants. Our Master washed His friends' feet. He went so far as to die so that others could live. Are we willing to follow Him to the cross?

Like obedience, service is something we offer up to God as an act of trust and love and worship. We serve because we love. We love Him, and we love those around us. Love, in fact, requires service. We serve our families. We serve our friends. We serve in organizations. We serve our churches. And as we serve others, we are actually serving the Lord.

Be obedient to those who are your masters according to the flesh, with fear and trembling, in sincerity of heart, as to Christ.

Describe how you are serving in this season of your life.
What changes, if any, would you make?

....

....

....

....

....

....

....

....

....

....

....

....

....

....

....

....

....

....

....

....

....

*Regardless of our status in life, each of
us has been chosen by God to serve
others and to live according to His Word.*

Service is what we provide when we see a need that we can meet and then meet it. Service is not limited to things that can be seen, recognized, or applauded in public. Service is every act of help or mercy we do for the glory of God.

Sometimes we can feel uninspired or burdened by the service we are involved in, especially if finances are tight or family obligations are stressful. If so, stop and think about the Lord's goodness in your life. Think about who you are. Realize you are God's chosen. You are a woman of influence in the King's royal court. Consider your service a way of saying thanks.

She opens her mouth with wisdom, and on her tongue
is the law of kindness.

PROVERBS 31:26

How does obedience and service intersect in your life?

Don't confuse doing things for God with doing things because you want to impress others.

The Lord requires us, as His disciples, to follow specific principles, and some of them are nonnegotiable. Here's one of them. When the Holy Spirit says go or stay, we are to obey Him. We have to learn to listen, and we have to be willing to do what we're told. God has designed us to accomplish different forms of service even though we might not see ourselves as the right person for the job. But that's God's decision, not ours.

Although God doesn't always call the qualified, He always qualifies the called. When God calls, He also equips. He uses the feeble things of this world to get His work done, and by doing that, He gets the greatest glory. Those looking on in amazement shake their heads and say, "It could only be God!"

Wait on the LORD; be of good courage, and He shall
strengthen your heart; wait, I say, on the LORD!

PSALM 27:14

*D*o you find it easy or difficult to serve? Why?

Be courageous and act with strength
and integrity when you serve.

*E*ven though God has gifted us with spiritual gifts that He intends for us to use in service to one another, investing our gifts by serving God's people feels risky. We are vulnerable to the possibility of rejection, criticism, or even failure. But it is only when we step out in faith and invest our gifts in His service that we are able to see the power of God at work and the blessing He has in store for us.

The Word of God tells us that each believer has a special role to play in the function of Christ's body. No one believer can do everything. When the body works together, God's program is propelled forward.

And He Himself gave some to be apostles, some prophets, some evangelists, and some pastors and teachers, for the equipping of the saints for the work of ministry, for the edifying of the body of Christ.

EPHESIANS 4:11-12

What gifts has God equipped you with to serve others? In what capacity are you using them?

....

....

....

....

....

....

....

....

....

....

....

....

....

....

....

....

....

....

....

....

....

....

....

....

....

....

....

....

....

....

....

....

....

....

....

....

*Sometimes the requests and obligations
we have to deal with drive us to our knees,
which is the best possible place to begin
our work.*

Once a session of service to God is over, we all need time to ourselves to find rest and recreation and retreat. God rested after He finished creating the world. Jesus went away to spend time alone with the Father. Should we do any less? Times of rest give us strength to complete the next task, accomplish more service, and enter a new season.

Stop for a moment. Listen carefully. Can you hear the voice of Jesus calling to you even now?

Come to Me, all you who labor and are heavy laden,
and I will give you rest.

MATTHEW 11:28

Do you take time to rest between seasons of service? What do you do to regain your strength?

Rest in the reality that God knows
what is best and will not withhold
any good thing from you.

Do you feel that life is standing still? Does it seem as if day after day nothing changes? Perhaps God is taking this time to prepare you for a special task or a future opportunity. Preparation, along with obedience and service, involves a time for cleansing, purifying, and anointing.

When we begin our walk with Jesus, His blood cleanses from all sin, and because of His holiness, we are declared holy too. But there are stains on our character that can lead us back into sin and failure. To remove our flaws, God cleanses us—the process is called "sanctification," and it goes on throughout our lives.

Therefore, my beloved, as you have always obeyed, not as in my
presence only, but now much more in my absence, work out your
own salvation with fear and trembling; for it is God who works in
you both to will and to do for His good pleasure.

PHILIPPIANS 2:12-13

When did you last spend time with the Lord for the specific purpose of sanctification?

....

....

....

....

....

....

....

....

....

....

....

....

....

....

....

....

....

*A*s we grow, an intense time of cleansing
is necessary before we fully enter into the
future He has planned for us.

The purification of our thoughts and motives is part of the cleansing process. Because we live in the world, we have learned certain patterns of thinking and acting that may not be in accordance with His will. God wants to transform our thought life, so that the motives that lie behind our actions will be pure and godly.

God also wants to anoint us for life in His kingdom. We need to utilize the anointing of the Holy Spirit so God can send us out into the world, ready and able to use the spiritual gifts He has given us. His desire is that our prayers and good works will drift into His presence like sweet-smelling incense.

May these words of my mouth and this meditation of my heart
be pleasing in your sight, Lord, my Rock and my Redeemer.

PSALM 19:14

*D*escribe the benefits of receiving God's anointing for future kingdom work.

....

....

....

....

....

....

....

....

....

....

....

....

....

....

....

....

....

....

....

....

....

....

....

....

....

....

....

....

....

....

....

....

....

....

....

We have to believe that God knows
what He is doing while we go through
the preparation process.

While God prepares you and it seems that time is standing still, it's helpful to remember whose we are and where we are. It is better to be standing still in His will than moving around at high speed outside of it.

God's timing is a mystery. And because He is a God of variety, your time of preparation and growth will be unlike that of anyone else's. To achieve your specific goals, you may need more education, spiritual growth, or insight. You may need to mature emotionally. Whatever it is we need to do, some of it will be done with the help of others, but most of it will be done in private.

The LORD is my shepherd; I shall not want. He makes me to lie
down in green pastures; He leads me beside the still waters.

PSALM 23:1-2

Whose business do you want to be involved with? Whose schedule are you on?

....

....

....

....

....

....

....

....

....

....

....

....

....

....

....

....

If you are on God's schedule,
you can rest in the knowledge that
He is in control, His timing is perfect,
and He doesn't make mistakes.

*I*f you want to have a full life in Christ, saturate yourself in His Word and steep yourself in prayer. Be prepared for whatever God has for you and learn to walk by faith.

As you abide in Him, you will naturally begin to think His thoughts. It is possible to be so close to the Savior that our thoughts are His thoughts and His ways are our ways. He wants us to look like Him. People should see us walking by and say, "There goes a disciple of Jesus Christ. She acts just like Him."

If you abide in Me, and My words abide in you, you will
ask what you desire, and it shall be done for you.

JOHN 15:7

What might people be saying about you as you live your Christian life?

_____

_____

_____

_____

_____

_____

_____

_____

_____

_____

_____

_____

_____

_____

_____

_____

_____

....

....

....

....

....

....

....

....

....

....

....

....

....

....

....

....

....

....

During the preparation time, you can fuss and fight or you can rest in the reality that He knows what is best and will not withhold any good thing from you.

The word "contentment" describes a feeling of satisfaction. It's realizing that after you have done all you can, you are able to rest in the awareness that God can complete His good work in your life without your help. He is not only your Savior, but He is your Good Shepherd. Your Savior will get you to heaven, but your Shepherd will give you the guidance and direction you need on earth. Contentment is a good thing, a godly thing.

But at times our contentment can lull us into a different experience—complacency. Complacency is a state of self-satisfaction or smugness. It takes our eyes off the Lord and His plans and His blessings. Beware of becoming complacent.

Godliness with contentment is great gain.

1 TIMOTHY 6:6 NIV

Share a time when contentment led you to complacency. What person or situation brought you out of your spiritual lethargy?

Contentment comes when you know your heavenly Father in an intimate, ongoing relationship.

We have to find a balance between finding contentment in difficult circumstances and becoming so comfortable in our surroundings that we refuse to get up, move forward, and fulfill God's plan.

Our commitments will stretch us. Sometimes they stretch us so far that our joy dries up. That's when we need to take inventory of what God has done for us in the past. We need to ask Him to give us our joy back as we worship Him. Tough commitments require us to develop a life of praise and worship. When praise becomes a habit, it is our lifeline. It is like a cable. We weave a thread of praise each day, and soon it becomes so strong we cannot break it.

I will rejoice in the LORD, I will joy in the God of my salvation.
The LORD God is my strength; He will make my feet like
deer's feet, and He will make me walk on my high hills.

HABAKKUK 3:18-19

What do you do when you are weary of the commitments you've made? How do you find the stamina to see them through to completion?

....

....

....

....

....

....

....

....

....

....

....

....

....

....

....

....

....

Contentment means that when you have done all that is within your power, you trust God with everything else.

Grace produces gratitude, and gratitude evokes service. If we really appreciate the grace of God, then we will seek opportunities to do things for Him.

When God graciously gives us opportunities, we must not become so comfortable as to grow content and allow complacency to rule our actions. As you face the everyday temptations to be selfish and think only of your personal peace and affluence, remember the goodness God has shown you. Make the commitment to leverage your position of grace for the benefit of God's kingdom.

Let us run with perseverance the race marked out for us, fixing
our eyes on Jesus, the pioneer and perfecter of faith.

HEBREWS 12:1-2 NIV

How does God show you grace? What is your response to His gift of grace?

....
....
....
....
....
....
....
....
....
....
....
....
....
....
....
....
....

If we hold on to Christ and let Him order
our steps, we can put His Word to action.

Although fear is a valid emotion, it is not effective when it begins to control us. If left unattended, fear can rob us of joy, immobilize us in our homes, and destroy our lives. The Bible reminds us that there is no fear in love; but perfect love—God's love for us—casts out fear.

The Bible also talks about an altogether different kind of fear—the fear of the Lord. It is good. It's the beginning of wisdom and knowledge. To fear God means to reverence Him, to hold Him in awe. That kind of godly fear leads to obedience because we realize the greatness of His power as well as His perfect love for us.

The fear of the LORD is the beginning of wisdom, and the
knowledge of the Holy One is understanding.

PROVERBS 9:10

Describe one of your biggest fears. Then search the Bible for a verse that speaks to that fear.

....
....
....
....
....
....
....
....
....
....
....
....
....
....
....
....
....
....
....

*O*ur minds—not our emotions—
need to set the course of our lives.

To overcome fear, fight it with the Word of God. This is a matter of the will. Fear often happens because of our lack of faith in God and our ignorance about His Word. The Lord has given us the capacity to overcome our fears by memorizing Scripture and quoting it when we're afraid.

Walk in the Spirit, not in the flesh. Realize that fear comes not only from the devil, but it also rises from the flesh. Heed the Bible and "walk in the Spirit, and you shall not fulfill the lust of the flesh. For the flesh lusts against the Spirit, and the Spirit against the flesh; and these are contrary to one another, so that you do not do the things that you wish" (Galatians 5:16-17).

Claim victory over fear every minute of the day. Every time you feel a twinge of fear, claim His promise: "I will never leave you nor forsake you" (Hebrews 13:5).

Take the helmet of salvation and the sword of the Spirit,
which is the word of God.

EPHESIANS 6:17 NIV

*M*emorize the Scripture you found in the previous devotion and use it to fight your fear. What are you learning about your fears?

....

....

....

....

....

....

....

....

....

....

....

....

....

....

....

....

....

....

....

Little faith will bring your soul to heaven;
great faith will bring heaven to your soul.

The Christian walk is a moment-by-moment walk, and we have to decide to whom we will yield our emotions. The Lord promises that if we call on Him, He is there to answer us. Recognize that in those times of despair, who has moved. Since He has not, it behooves us to once again draw near to Him.

Focusing on the sovereign nature and perfect purposes of our eternal God allows us to regain control of our emotions and find godly wisdom and confidence in every situation. When we place our confidence in Him, our lives become inexpressibly more relaxed and comfortable.

He Himself has said, "I will never leave you nor forsake you."

Are you beginning to feel less fearful? Why or why not?

The time spent dwelling on the
negative should, instead, be spent
dwelling on His promises.

Sometimes we do not see God working in our lives. When we enter into God's presence by fasting and praying, our prayers are instilled with more power. By sacrificing the physical to gain spiritual power, we can overcome the circumstances and burdens in our lives.

It's important to realize that you do not have to do all the praying by yourself. The life of faith is not intended to be lived alone. Reach out and support one another with intercessory prayer and bear the other's burdens in prayers of petition. When you get to a point where you just want out, when you don't feel that you have what it takes to accomplish your mission, call on as many godly people as possible to fast and pray. Once you do that, expect to see His power unleashed and His will accomplished in your circumstances.

....

....

....

....

....

....

....

....

....

....

....

....

....

....

....

....

....

....

Go, gather all the Jews who are present in Shushan,
and fast for me; neither eat nor drink for three days,
night or day. My maids and I will fast likewise.

ESTHER 4:16

*A*re you willing to entrust yourself to God, even when it takes you out of your comfort zone?

....

....

....

....

....

....

....

....

....

....

....

....

....

....

....

....

....

....

....

....

....

....

....

....

....

....

....

....

....

....

....

....

....

....

....

....

*God takes good care of His own.
It's up to us to pray and fast,
trust and obey while He does His work.*

*L*iving in our seasons requires us to learn lessons in patience. Sometimes we grow weary of the responsibilities and their requirements and become anxious to move on. When God hasn't yet told us to move on, the word "patience" takes on a whole new meaning.

Remember these truths and be encouraged: God has a purpose—and many blessings that accompany that purpose—for us in the seasons of our lives; He is sovereign, and nothing comes into our lives without His approval; He has promised to supply all our needs through Jesus; and we can turn to fellow believers for prayer and comfort.

As seasons come and go, we develop patience in the wake of learning what it means to trust and love the Lord.

And we know that all things work together for good to those who love God, to those who are the called according to His purpose.

ROMANS 8:28

In what way is your ability to be patient being stretched in this season? What joys are you discovering in this same season?

....
....
....
....
....
....
....
....
....
....
....
....
....
....
....
....
....

When we allow God to work in our lives
according to His plans, according to the
seasons of His choosing, we find that
salvation has come to our house.

*M*ove yourself away from the distractions and position yourself in the stillness of His presence. In every season of a woman's life, God's presence is critical to living out that season to the fullest. Give Him a call. Jeremiah 33:3 says, "Call to Me and I will answer you, and I will tell you great and mighty things, which you do not know."

I encourage you to refresh your mind with God's viewpoint rather than your own, use this time as a season of expecting a spiritual and physical renewal, keep praying and praising, speak good things into your life, and focus on God's perfect timing. Fully maximize your life in the season that God has you in.

These things I have spoken to you, so that in Me you may have peace. In the world you have tribulation, but take courage, I have overcome the world.

JOHN 16:33

What changes are you making to help endure this season
of your life?

....

....

....

....

....

....

....

....

....

....

....

....

....

....

....

....

....

....

When you find Him, you will find His
strength, His might, and His power.

*R*emember that Jesus will move closer to us if we let Him. He is our comfort, and He does have a plan for each of us. Jesus doesn't promise that every season of your life will be without turbulence or trouble, but He does promise to lead you safely to the destination He has planned for you.

Don't get caught up on where you are or the struggles you face. You are in a chosen season right now, and you have wonderful seasons up ahead. As a passionate and persistent woman of God, stay focused on Him. Remain determined and connected, and He will walk with you through each and every season of your life.

I lift up my eyes to the mountains—where does my help come from? My help comes from the Lord, the Maker of heaven and earth.

Psalm 121:1-2 NIV

What have you learned that helps you prepare now
for your next season?

....

....

....

....

....

....

....

....

....

....

....

....

....

....

....

....

....

....

....
....
....
....
....
....
....
....
....
....
....
....
....
....
....
....
....
....

*Your safest place is in the
center of God's will.*

When our mouth was filled with laughter,
and our tongue with singing...

The LORD has done great things for us,
and we are glad.

PSALM 126:2-3